# Ben Clarke
# Rugby Skills

# Ben Clarke's Rugby Skills

# A Complete Step-by-Step Guide

**Specially commissioned photography by Action Plus**

HAMLYN

**Acknowledgements**
There are many people to thank for their help in putting this book together. In particular I would like to thank David Lawrenson for helping me put my ideas into words so skilfully and to Bath FC for the use their ground for the photographic shoot. I am also grateful to Gareth Adams of Bath FC for his help on the field during the shoot; to John Palmer of King Edward's School, Bath for bringing some outstanding schoolboy players to the shoot; to Derek de Glanville of Rhino Rugby Ltd for bringing scrummaging equipment to the shoot; to Puma UK for the use of their text and pictures in the fitness section; and to Tony Pocock and Ashley Western for their help at various stages of the book's production.

**Picture Acknowledgements**
Front cover: Allsport/David Cannon main picture
Allsport/Shaun Botterill 33, 63 top, /Howard Boyland 46 top, David Cannon 12 bottom, 15 top, 15 bottom, 45, 49 bottom, 62 bottom, /Russell Cheyne 31 top, 31 bottom, 55, /Phil Cole 34 top, /Andrew Cornaga 25 top, /John Gichigi 60, /Mike Hewitt 54, 61 bottom, /David Rogers 1, 2, 8 top, 12 top, 13, 14, 17 bottom, 50/51 bottom, 51 right, 61 top, 63 bottom, /Billy Stickland 62 top, /Anton Want 6, 19 bottom, 37; Mark Leech 22; Puma 58 top right, 58 top left, 58 bottom right, 59 top left, 59 bottom left, 59 centre left, 59 top right, 59 bottom right.

First published in Great Britain in 1995 by Hamlyn, an imprint of Reed Consumer Books Limited, Michelin House, 81 Fulham Road, London SW3 6RB, and Auckland, Melbourne, Singapore and Toronto

Copyright © 1995 Reed International Books Limited

ISBN 0 600 58511 5

A catalogue record of this book is available from the British Library.

Project Editor: Adam Ward
Art Editor: Keith Martin
Design: Paul Carpenter
Picture Researcher: Jenny Faithful
Production Controller: Michelle Thomas

Printed and bound in Hong Kong by Mandarin Offset.

# Contents

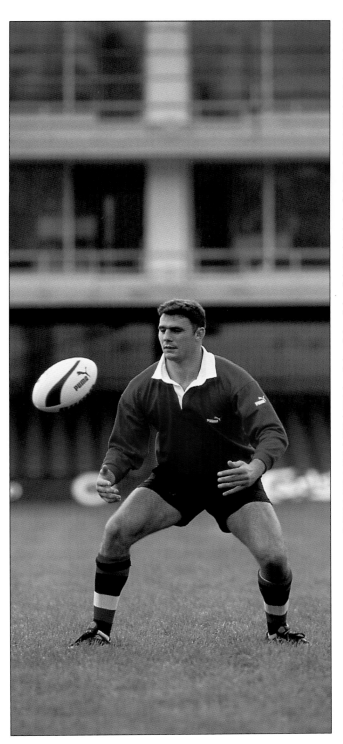

# Introduction

Not surprisingly, I believe that rugby is the greatest game in the world. It's terrific to play because it combines skill with strength; and while it is often a physical contest it can also produce moments of sheer magic for the players.

It is a game for all shapes and sizes, so there's room for a Jeremy Guscott, a Jason Leonard and a Martin Bayfield in the same team. It can also be played, and is played, at a variety of levels throughout the country so anyone, regardless of size or skill, can enjoy it on a regular basis.

But the wonderful thing about rugby is not only the pleasure it gives through playing the game but also the friendships and camaraderie it generates off the field; and this is true at whatever level you play. The team spirit that the game engenders is enormous and, no matter how hard fought the contest, the idea of shaking hands with your opponents and clapping each other off the field is enshrined in the whole ethos of the game.

Not everyone can be an international player or play at a high level. But everyone can improve their game with coaching. Of course, this is best done on the training pitch under the watchful eye of a knowledgeable coach. But that's not always possible so I hope that the skills and practices in this book will help the developing player to understand rugby better and will serve as an aid to improving his game.

There is no doubt that I have benefited greatly from the work of several dedicated coaches during my career – in particular, Chris Davis, Tony Russ, Jack Rowell and Ian McGeechan. But not everyone can rely on expert tuition from an early age, which is why I have tried to cover in this book all facets of play, all positions on the field and what is expected from each. Even if you are a back, I hope it will unravel some of the mysteries of forward play and vice versa. If this book helps your overall understanding of the game a little, or develops your play, then it will have served a more than useful purpose.

There is no doubt that some people are born with more natural talent than others but it is amazing what can be achieved by someone less talented but with a bit of commitment and a lot of practice. It is no accident that the best goalkickers in the world are invariably the ones who spend the most time practising their kicking and the best line-out jumpers are the ones who work hardest on it in training.

But never forget that rugby has to be enjoyable. Even at the highest level, if we didn't enjoy playing the game we simply would not go out there and play every Saturday. And you'll enjoy the game even more if you spend as much time as you can practising and working on your skills. I guarantee it!

# Coaching

**F**or a long time rugby didn't bother with coaches. Instead, players relied on the captain to organise the team and the training sessions. But as the game became more popular and grew more competitive, the value of having a specialist who could get the best out of the team and its players became increasingly obvious.

These days every team has a coach, from mini and youth rugby through to clubs at every level of excellence and to international teams as well. Some coaches have become famous in their own right, such as Bob Dwyer of the present world champions, Australia. Most have played the game to a high level, but you don't have to be a star player to be a successful coach. Jack Rowell, of Bath and now England, is one of the most successful coaches in the country, but he never played the game at international level. Coaching is all about communication – being able to convey ideas to players in a way that they can understand. The most gifted player in the world will

Jack Rowell, Ben's coach at Bath and now the highly successful England coach.

**A coach must be able to analyse and assess the strengths and weaknesses of each player he is coaching. Here Ben gives advice on how to receive a pass.**

**Coaching is all about communication. Here Ben sums up the lessons learned after a morning's coaching session.**

not make a good coach if he cannot explain properly to players what he wants them to do.

Obviously the coach must have a good knowledge of the game, and especially of the skills and techniques needed for every position on the field. He must be able to analyse and assess each player he is coaching and pick out his strengths and weaknesses. He must then be able to work on those weaknesses so the player can improve his game. A coach must also have the right personality. He must be able to gain the confidence of his players so that they will accept his teaching without question. The attitude of a coach must be constructive. He must set achievable goals for his team and strive always to devise a positive game-plan for every match they play.

It should be the coach's job to organise the training, both stamina work and individual skills, as well as team skills and tactics.

More and more these days, a coach will bring in a specialist to concentrate on a particular area. For instance, Rob Andrew, the England fly-half, works on his kicking skills with coach Dave Alred. A coach might recruit someone to take charge of fitness routines, or bring in an expert on scrummaging or line-out work. Far from diluting his authority, such appointments show that the coach is actively thinking about what is best for his team. Bringing in new faces for specific work is always a good idea because even the best of coaches can get stale and players can grow a little weary of hearing the same voice and

doing the same drills all the time at training sessions.

Coaching is a two-way thing. A coach should always be prepared to listen to what a player has to say and go along with his suggestions if he thinks they are worthwhile. A successful coach will always have a good relationship with his captain – as exists between Bob Dwyer and Michael Lynagh – because when it comes to the game, it is the captain who takes charge out on the field; the coach must watch from the sidelines.

Coaches have a tremendous responsibility in the modern game. Their work, particularly with younger players, is vital in shaping the rugby players of tomorrow, and not just in developing their technical skills, but also in their attitude to the team and to the game.

# Principles of play

Rugby is one of the great team games. Although individual skills are essential, a team can only be effective when the whole side is functioning as a unit. Notable examples of this are the Welsh team of the 1970s, New Zealand during the late 1980s and the current Auckland and Bath sides.

The requirements of each position on the field are so diverse that everyone can be accommodated. Rugby is definitely a game for all shapes and sizes but it is also about individual attributes and skills. A boy may not have the best hand-to-eye co-ordination but he may be a strong tackler or a powerful scrummager and, as such, valuable

team member. Commitment and heart also count for a lot on the rugby field.

Youngsters don't always end up in the position in which they first play, so here's a run-down of all the positions in a team and what is expected of each. Don't be afraid to change positions in your search for the one which suits you best.

A full-back must tackle well. Often he is the last line of defence and must stop the ball carrier who has time and space on his side.

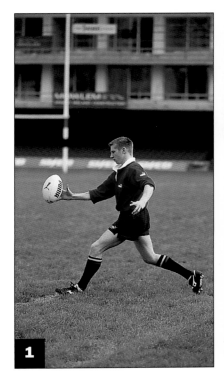

**1**

A full-back must be a good kicker of the ball out of hand. He will often need to clear his lines with a long punt.

**2**

Many full-backs use a screw-kick to kick for touch – the ball is kicked at a slight angle and rotates in flight.

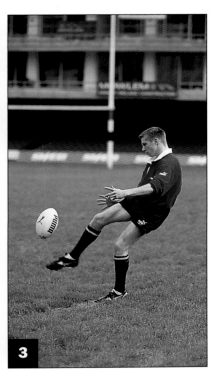

**3**

Hold the ball at an angle, then hit it with the outside of your boot, keep your head down and make clean contact.

## Full-back

There used to be a time when the full-back was just a defensive player, the last line of defence. That has all changed now because in the modern game he has become a potent attacking force. Some believe that the full-back can be the most dangerous attacker on the field.

The full-back position is unique in that it is the only one that is isolated. If you play there, often there is no one next to you to gee you up and give you confidence, so you need to be a strong character as well as a strong player. Serge Blanco and Gavin Hastings typify the full-back position.

Often you will be making decisions which will be crucial to the team and, because of your isolated position, you are constantly under the microscope. If one of the forwards or one of the inside backs misses a tackle, it may not be crucial, as there will usually be time for somebody else to cover. But when a full-back misses a tackle everybody can see the danger immediately and often it leads to a try.

A good positional sense is the first requirement if you want to play full-back. That means that you must be able to read the game well and position yourself as it unfolds, ready for any eventuality. For example, if you have noticed that the opposition fly-half is mainly a one-footed kicker, you can work out, in certain situations, to which part of the field he is likely to kick the ball.

A full-back must be a good kicker of the ball out of the hand, and be a sound tackler. Timing a tackle is especially important for a full-back because often you will have to stop a ball carrier who has both time and space in which to beat you. Courage is needed to make tackles on big forwards as well as speedy backs. Sound technique is needed in fielding high balls. It is essential to concentrate on catching the ball, while ignoring the distracting attentions of the chasers who will be breathing down your neck.

Above all, at full-back you are a potentially devastating attacker. John Gallagher, the former New Zealand full-back, is a fine example, adding an extra dimension to the team's attacking play. So if you have speed and good handling ability, develop the knack of knowing when to enter the three-quarter line and practise with the three-quarters. If you time your entry well, no defence will touch you.

When we think of a wing we automatically think of speed: Tony Underwood (above), for example, or his brother Rory (below). The latter is seen here leaving his marker for dead as he streaks for the line in a Five Nations match against Scotland.

## Wing

When we think of the wing three-quarter positions we automatically think of speed and, in particular, such exciting players as David Campese, the Australian winger who was voted Player of the Tournament in the 1991 World Cup. Of course, wings have to have pace because they are the finishers, the try-scorers. Often chances will be few and far between, so every one must be taken and an extra yard of speed can make the difference between scoring and being bundled into touch short of the line.

You can work on your basic speed but you should also have other ways of beating a man. Work on your side step and swerve as well as change of pace. Above all, don't just stay out on your wing and wait for the ball to come to you. Get involved.

**Centres come in all shapes and sizes but essentially you are the team's link man – the creator. You must have good handling skills and be able to give and take a pass in one smooth movement. Jeremy Guscott is one of the world's great centres.**

Think about your position and try to vary the angles of your runs. Keep your opposite number guessing. When you're in an attacking formation, say at a line-out or at a scrum, don't always line up directly opposite your opposing wing whose task is to mark you. Try standing inside him to take a short pass off your centre; then on the next occasion stand outside him with your centre making a longer pass. This will keep your opponent guessing and he will be wary of you. But always tell your centre what you are going to do. Don't keep him guessing, too!

Also, a wing has a lot of defensive duties to carry out, and must often act as a cover for the full-back, so make sure that your kicking and positional play are up to scratch.

If you see a try-scoring opportunity, go for it. It takes courage to go for the corner when all the cover is converging on you at great speed, but all the great wingers I have played with have had the courage to take up the challenge and have succeeded.

## Centre

Centre three-quarters come in all kinds of shapes and sizes but the requirements remain the same. Essentially, as a centre you're a link man, a creator. You must have good handling skills and be able to give and take a pass in one smooth movement.

We tend to look for spectacular breaks from centres – and there are few more spectacular than Jeremy Guscott, of Bath and England, when in full cry – but there is much more

to it than that. Many centres get as much enjoyment out of creating an opening for their wing through a pass or a half-break as they do in scoring themselves.

You must be a good tackler and be prepared for a lot of head-on tackling. It is also a position which requires subtlety, knowing when to pass and when to break.

Centres must have good positional sense and know how to straighten a line. When the ball is passed out from the scrum-half to the fly-half, there is a tendency for these players and then the centre to run at an angle towards the corner-flag. If this is allowed to continue, by the time the ball reaches the wing he will have run out of space. So the centre must be aware of this and straighten up the line if he feels it is drifting. ➡

## ➡ Fly-half

As the key playmaker in any team, the fly-half must have all the skills plus a cool head and a shrewd rugby brain. Kicking, particularly out of defence, is as important as speed off the mark and good handling skills. But all that will mean nothing if he cannot make key decisions quickly and choose the right option.

As a fly-half, therefore, never be afraid to experiment and always be prepared to change tactics if something is not working. I am reminded of Stuart Barnes's electrifying run through the centre, setting up Guscott and then Underwood to score a try, in the 1993 Scotland v England international. If you change tactics and the new plan still does not work out, then at least you know you have tried. There is nothing worse or more frustrating for your team-mates than persisting with the same tactic or game plan when it's plainly not working.

You have to be confident in your own ability because a lot rests on your shoulders. Be clear in your own mind what you want to do, and in training sessions work out what your options are wherever the play is on the field so, when it comes to a match, you will know instinctively what choices you have. It is then just a matter of making the right one.

## Scrum-half

This is the most involved position of all on a rugby pitch. A good scrum-half – and few have been better than Nick Farr-Jones, captain of the 1991 Australian World Cup-winning side – must be skilful and combative. Together with the fly-half, he is one of the chief decision-makers on the pitch. Indeed, he is the prime decision-maker, choosing whether to pass the ball out from set pieces, or go on his own, or kick, or take it on with the forwards.

The fly-half is the key playmaker in any team – for England, Rob Andrew fills this role. He is an outstanding kicker and is England's leading points scorer.

A good scrum-half must be combative as well as skilful. Dewi Morris filled that role for England for a number of years before giving way to Kyran Bracken.

The pass is obviously a key element of the scrum-half's skills and being able to pass off either hand is essential. But some scrum-halves become obsessed with the length of their pass: that is much less important than speed. So if you play scrum-half, remember it's no use having a super long pass if it takes you so long to deliver it that it arrives with your fly-half at the same time as the opposition's defences.

The scrum-half is an essential link with the forwards and in many situations acts as their eyes and ears.

## No.8

A dynamic player, always involved both in attack and defence, the No.8's position at the base of the scrum means that he forms a link with the scrum-half and is the pivot for many back-row moves. No.8s in the modern game must also contribute to the line-out and so need to be big, strong and excellent jumpers.

Defensively, the No.8 acts like a flanker but in attack he is usually looking to exploit gaps and therefore has to be a powerful and athletic runner. In the thick of the action all the time, he will be one of the fittest players in the team. And remember: if you play No.8 you also need good positional sense and tactical awareness, and you would do well to emulate the outstanding Australian No.8, Tim Gavin.

The No.8 is a dynamic player, always involved in attack and defence. Ben feels particularly at home in that position, as in this photograph from an England v Scotland Five Nations match.

## ➡ Flanker

The flanker's most important attribute is his ability to tackle. He is essentially a destroyer who harrasses the opposing backs, particularly the scrum-half and fly-half. An ability to reach any breakdown in play quickly and secure the ball is essential, and for this he needs pace as well as courage. In January 1995 I enjoyed one of my best games for England playing at flanker and scoring against Ireland.

Angles of running and a good positional sense are other attributes a good flanker must acquire. He will also be required to support any breaks by the backs and be available if an attack peters out.

Most teams play with an open-side flanker and a blind-side flanker, the blind-side being the narrower side of the pitch at a scrum. As the game has developed, the two flankers have evolved quite distinct roles. The blind-side flanker is usually physically bigger and more powerful for a role that is essentially defensive, while the open-side flanker is the out-and-out flyer, the man with real pace who can track the opposition backs and harry them into making mistakes. Both have contributions to make to the line-out, with the blind-side flanker usually taking up a position in the middle and the open-side at the tail ready to home in on the opposition fly-half if the ball is lost.

The alternative to playing open-side and blind-side flankers is to play left and right flankers, where both get a chance of playing open-side and blind-side, and that really depends on the individual skills and attributes of the two players.

## Lock

The most important role for a lock today is in the line-out because there

The scrum is set with the No.8 at the base of the scrum, the two locks in front of him and the flankers positioned on either side.

are so many line-outs in a match. But locks also have an essential job to do in the scrum so if you play there you will need height as well as strength and power. Athletic ability and handling skills are also increasingly necessary as part of a lock's repertoire, for while the physical demands of line-out work and scrummaging are immense, locks today are expected to get around and contribute to all aspects of play.

The locks usually divide into front and middle jumpers at the line-out. The front jumper is not usually as tall as the middle jumper and wins the ball as much by guile

and timing as by jumping higher than his opponent – England's Martin Johnson exemplifies this.

But locks must be flexible when it comes to the line-out and must also be prepared to take a lot of buffeting. As a lock you will certainly be expected to do your best to deny the opposition possession as well as secure the ball for your own side.

## Prop

Props need to be very strong in the upper body, particularly around the neck and shoulders. Propping makes tremendous physical demands on a player. If you play prop you are

**The hooker has struck for the ball which is now being channelled back through the forest of legs to the scrum-half.**

constantly locked in combat with your opposite number, so you must be mentally as well as physically tough. Props are divided into loose-head and tight-head.

The loose-head appears on the left of the scrum where the ball is put in by his scrum-half. His objective is to make things easy for his hooker by ensuring the ball can be won cleanly.

The tight-head prop is the anchor of the scrum. He has to remain solid and unmovable and must withstand whatever pressure is imposed by the opposition when they try to wheel the scrum round and disrupt it.

Props have essential roles in ruck and maul and are used as blockers and supports in the line-out.

## Hooker

The hooker, like the prop, must be strong in the neck and shoulders but will probably be leaner and more mobile than the props. Winning his own ball in the scrum is vital. His other task is to throw in at the line-out, so being able to throw accurately is essential.

If you play hooker you will be expected to contribute in loose play, so you must have good handling skills, and you must also be mobile. My England team-mate Brian Moore is one of the best hookers in world rugby and has all these qualities in abundance.

**The England front row, props Jeff Probyn and Jason Leonard and hooker Brian Moore, against New Zealand in the 1991 World Cup curtain raiser.**

# Running with the ball

nyone's list of the top ten rugby players of all time will be dominated by those who are or were great runners. Contemporary candidates include Simon Geoghegan and the aptly named Tony Swift. Everyone who plays rugby yearns to run with the ball in the hand: even a prop or lock forward invariably earns a huge cheer when he sets off on a run.

Everyone can run with a ball but to some it comes naturally – notably, the exciting French team on a surging counter-attack. However, do not despair if you are not one of these: it is possible to work on your style and correct a bad technique. The important thing is to develop a rhythm in your running: lean forward slightly, pick up your knees and try to achieve a comfortable stride pattern. There is more about sprinting on page 55.

You should try to hold the ball out in front of you, although if you are a wing or a full-back or are making a break for the line you are more likely to hold it under one arm. This should be the arm furthest away from any would-be tackler so you can use your free arm to fend him off.

Developing a good running style that maximises your potential is something you can do on your own. Start to think about your running and develop a rhythm. More often than not, you will be faced by tacklers intent on stopping your progress so you must learn ways to beat them – pace alone will not always be enough. There are several methods including the side-step, swerve and change in pace.

## The Side-step

It is often said that you can't teach anyone to side-step: either you've got it or you haven't. There is some truth in this: some players are just natural side-steppers, although with practice you can certainly bring out an ability that perhaps you did not think you had.

**Develop a rhythm in your running and hold the ball in both hands in front of you. If you hold the ball in one hand and on the hip (see left) you can't make a pass and the ball will be lost immediately in a tackle.**

The mechanics of the side-step are as follows: if, for example, you are side-stepping off your right foot, you should carry the ball in your right hand and lean over to the right as you approach your opponent. Just before you get to him you drive hard off your right foot to the left and then sprint away.

The same process works in reverse to side-step off your left foot. Most people are stronger off one foot, but talented players can side-step both ways, so try to develop your weaker

**Selling a dummy is an effective way to beat a defender. The aim is to kid him that you are going to pass rather than break.**

**Anticipating a tackle from an All Blacks' defender, during the Lions' tour of 1993, I hold the ball in my left arm and prepare to hand off with my right.**

side. Timing is important because if you side-step too early your opponent will have time to adjust and be able to tackle you. If you side-step too late, you will be too close and once again he may be able to tackle you.

Develop the timing for a side-step by trial and error until it is instinctive. The beauty of the side-step is that it can be done in a relatively confined space and, when executed well, it will take you clear of your opponent.

## The Swerve

Everyone can be taught to swerve and, although the side-step is the more common method of beating an opponent, a well-executed swerve can be even more effective. The swerve is an essential part of a winger's armoury but a player in any position who finds himself in space with an opponent to beat should consider using it.

The swerve involves running straight at your opponent at pace, which means that he will have to set himself up in a particular spot to tackle you. He cannot move left or right for fear of leaving you a gap to go through.

If an opponent is coming across the pitch to tackle you, by heading for him you will force him to stop for fear of over-running you. Once you have forced him to stop, if you are swerving to the left you need to use a sharp cross step with the right foot, the rest of your body will follow and suddenly you are on a different angle going away from the tackler.

The advantage of the swerve is that you are moving at pace all the time and when you are going past your opponent you should be at full speed whereas he will be trying to match you from virtually a standing start. The other point about the swerve is that it takes you away from the other defenders who will be coming across the pitch to try to cut you off.

The hand-off is important with the swerve because, if you go a little too close to the tackler, a fend with your inside arm, given your momentum, can mean the difference between being tackled and getting away. Make sure you carry the ball in the outside arm to facilitate the hand off.

## Change of pace

It is important, particularly if you are a three-quarter, to be able to change pace easily. A well executed change of pace can fool even the best defender. Practise going at a defender at just below full speed and then just as he's lined you up and is committing himself to the tackle, hit top speed and accelerate past him and away.

# Passing

**1**

**The key elements in passing are the wrists and fingertips.**

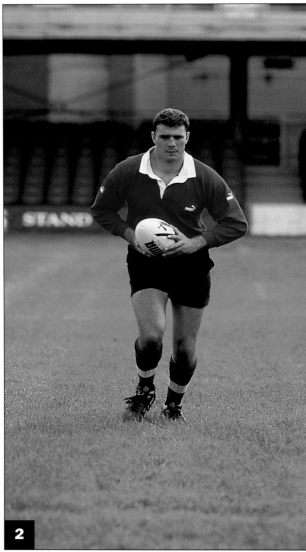

**2**

**The ball must feel comfortable in your hands.**

When various forms of football were being developed about a hundred and fifty years ago, what set rugby football apart from the others was that it was a handling game. Association football developed into a purely kicking game but ever since William Webb Ellis, one day at Rugby School, picked up the ball and ran with it, the rugby code has been associated with handling and passing the ball by hand.

Passing movements bring the greatest satisfaction to both players and spectators, and few who saw it can forget the magnificent French passing counter-attack which led to a try against New Zealand in 1994. There was a time when only backs concentrated on their handling skills, but in the modern game forwards are expected to have good handling skills, too. They are encouraged to develop their skills so that they can give and take a pass.

Passing is simply an effective method of transferring the ball over distance. Done properly, the ball can be moved down a line quicker than a player can run, so the advantages on the rugby field are obvious.

Handling should become second nature, and you should work on it until it is an integral part of your game. Remember, of course, that you cannot pass the ball forward so there are certain guidelines which have to be followed.

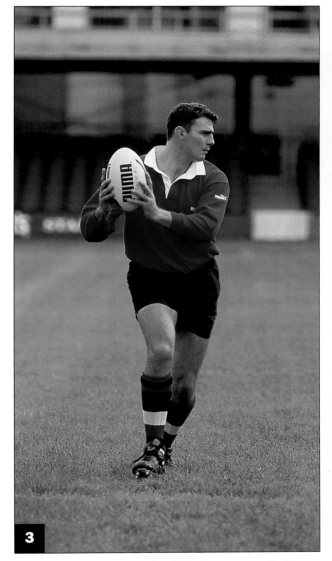

**3**

Before making the pass, swing the ball across your body.

**4**

Propel the ball at your team-mate using your fingers and wrists.

## Ben's tips

● The ball must feel comfortable in your hands before you make a pass.

● Deliver the ball as you would wish to receive it – at chest height, perfectly weighted and slightly in front of the receiver.

● Don't hold the ball too close to your chest before passing it as this will waste time.

The key elements in passing are the wrists and the fingertips. The ball must feel comfortable in your hands before you swing it across your body and then propel it with your fingers and wrists. You need to direct the ball at chest height to the player you are passing to and slightly in front of him so that he doesn't lose any momentum when trying to catch the ball. The perfect pass is one that is at a comfortable height, is perfectly weighted, and

doesn't cause the catcher to lose speed or change direction.

If you are transferring the ball, simply swing your wrists across your body and let it go. Don't be tempted to hug the ball into your chest before passing it on, for this will only take up precious time and may cause the move to break down. Just say to yourself 'catch and pass' and let it go in one movement. The more you practise, the easier it will become until it is a natural action.

# Catching

When taking a pass, the catcher must present the passer with a target. He should hold his hands out by his chest with the palms facing where the ball is coming from. Always keep your eyes on the ball no matter what is happening around you because a split second's distraction will cause you to drop the ball.

Sometimes the catcher will have to take a spin pass, though spin passes generally should be avoided unless used over a particularly long distance. Even the best spin passer needs to adjust the ball slightly and this takes time which is valuable. Spin passes also need slightly more time to take and usually need some adjustment to be made on the part of the receiver. Once again these split seconds are vital and can mean the difference between a player being put clear and being tackled.

Of course, in a game like rugby one can never expect perfect passes all the time. When under pressure, passes come to the catcher at all angles and at all heights but the method of taking them is the same. If it is a low pass then you should bend your knees to make it easier.

You should practise taking passes at different heights and also short and long passes. Remember, possession is everything and a lot of hard work may have gone into winning that particular ball, so don't let the team down by dropping it.

Gavin Hastings, Scotland's full-back and captain, catches a high ball perfectly in the 1992 Scotland v Wales Five Nations match.

## Ben's tips

● Present the passer with a target — hold your hands with the palms facing the ball.

● Keep your eyes fixed on the ball. Don't be distracted by anything that is going on around you.

● When taking a high ball, turn your body side-on to protect yourself against opponents.

## Taking a high ball

One specific area of catching which does require a different technique is the fielding of a high ball. Although this task usually falls to full-backs and wings, all players should know how to take a high ball.

An advantage in catching the high ball is that you have time to set yourself to receive it. It is essential that you keep your eyes on the ball, turn side-on to give yourself some protection against opponents who may be coming through to challenge, and raise your hands upwards with fingers outstretched, directed towards the ball. You then pull the ball into your body and secure it.

**1**

**The catcher can help the passer by presenting him with a target. He should hold out his hands by his chest with the palms facing where the ball is coming from, keeping his eyes firmly on the ball (see pictures above and below).**

**2**

You must keep your eyes fixed on the ball and ignore what is going on around you. Putting up a high kick to test the full-back and allow the chasers to put pressure on him is an increasingly popular tactic. Taking these high balls, often called 'garryowens' after the Irish club which popularised their use, calls for real concentration because you will be under extreme pressure as the ball comes down.

But if you have got your technique right – keeping your eyes fixed on the ball and resisting the temptation to look at the oncoming players – you should have no problem in dealing with it.

# Tackling

Rugby is a physical contact sport and tackling plays a major part in it. You cannot hope to play a full part in the game and be successful if you cannot tackle. It is probably the aspect of the game that youngsters are most apprehensive about but the fact is that if your technique is right then you are unlikely to get hurt. You may even come to enjoy tackling; indeed, there is something very satisfying about dumping your opponent on the ground.

The most important element in tackling is confidence. It is important for the coach to build up confidence in young players by teaching the right technique and beginning slowly and simply.

Tackling is essentially about halting the progress of the ball carrier and the best way to do this is to tackle him around the legs – he can't go anywhere without them! However, good tackling does not depend on size. The best tacklers are often the more lightly built players, such as Peter Winterbottom, and there is tremendous satisfaction in bringing down an opponent who is bigger than you are.

In a game you will be called on to make several different types of tackle as players will come at you from different directions and in a variety of situations. The main tackles are the side tackle, the front-on tackle and the tackle from behind. All follow the same basic principles.

## The Side tackle

This is probably the simplest type of tackle. Use this tackle when a player is shaping up to go past you. Line him up and hit him at 90 degrees to the line of his run. It is important to put your head behind his legs as you make contact and aim to drive in with your shoulder around the thighs. You then wrap your arms around his

**The side tackle. I have lined up my opponent and begin my run at him.**

**My run is well timed, so my head and shoulders drive in behind his legs.**

**My opponent is floored by the momentum of my tackle.**

legs and his forward momentum will force him to the ground.

The position of the head cannot be overemphasised. Make sure it's behind the thighs and you won't have any problems. Timing is important, so you should make sure that your eyes are open and focused on the area you're going to hit. If you go too high and end up around his hips, the ball carrier can easily shrug you off. Similarly, going too low around the ankles will not be as effective and can be dangerous for the tackler. Once you have decided to take the ball carrier out with a tackle from the side, you should be fully committed and must not hesitate. If you do, you'll probably miss the man.

## The Front-on tackle

Psychologically, the front-on tackle is probably the most difficult because the ball carrier is running at you and your alternatives are either to jump out of the way or to let him run straight over you – neither of which I would recommend!

However, the principles remain the same as before, so if you can tackle from the side then you can certainly tackle front-on. The most important point, once again, is the position of the head. This time you will be looking to put your head to one side of his legs.

Again, you should drive your shoulder into his thighs and wrap

**Lee Stensness, the All Blacks' centre, is tackled from the side by an Australian defender in the 1993 Bledisloe Cup match and is forced to part with the ball. Note the position of the tackler's head.**

your arms around them – because of his momentum you will end up on top of him (see pictures 1 and 2 below).

Timing is important, and you should try to move towards him if you can. It will be easier to tackle him before he has reached his full speed; and if you are static yourself it will be easier for him to go round you.

Taking the initiative in the front-on tackle is crucial because there is simply no time for hesitation. Be decisive and you will be very effective. Make it a matter of personal pride. You gain a major psychological advantage when your opponent realises that he can't run straight through you.

**Position your head to the side of your opponent's legs, wrap your arms around his thighs and drive in with your shoulder.**

⇒ **The Tackle from behind**

All the same principles apply to the tackle from behind. This time you put your head to one side of the ball carrier's legs and drive in with your shoulder around the top of his thighs. Again, because of his momentum and the force of your hit, you should finish up on top of him.

The tackle from behind: move confidently into the tackling position. Hesitancy at this point results in a failed tackle, so be decisive.

When you drive your shoulders into your opponent's thighs, you must use enough force to halt his run and send him to the ground.

On this occasion I have timed my tackle correctly, bringing my opponent to the floor and finishing up on top of him.

## The Smother tackle

Sometimes you will be called on to make a smother tackle, which means wrapping your arms around the ball carrier at chest height to prevent him from passing the ball. Although the smother tackle may be necessary in certain situations during match play, it is not really a method which should be encouraged in youngsters, although as you progress in the game you will find this tackle increasingly valuable.

To begin with, there is a danger that you will go too high and anything around the neck or head is an illegal tackle and will be severely penalised. Also, trying to tackle a player moving at pace high up on the chest is asking for trouble. More often than not you will simply bounce off. How many times have you heard commentators, after a try has been scored, saying that the would-be tacklers 'went too high'. Leave the smother tackle for specific situations at close quarters.

The smother tackle: wrap your arms around your opponent's chest to stop him passing.

## Tackle bags

Most clubs and schools these days have tackle bags which are a tremendous help in training. It is great to be able to cut loose on them and they provide an important confidence-building exercise. Just charge at them and hit them as hard as you can.

Once you've made sure you've got your technique right, arrange to have the bags moving to enable you to work on your timing and co-ordination. As soon as you feel confident, start to work with a partner. Try the side tackle first: have your partner walk along the touchline and then come in from the side to make the tackle. When you've got that right, get him to jog slowly, gradually speeding up until he's running. Then do the same for the front-on tackle and the tackle from behind.

Tackle bags are a tremendous help in training. Just charge and hit them as hard as you can.

## Ben's tips

● Perfect your tackling technique and build confidence by practising with tackle bags.

● The position of the head is crucial. Put your head behind the opponent's legs when tackling from the side, and place it to one side of the legs when tackling from behind or front-on.

● Don't hesitate. Be confident and committed.

# Attacking play

All teams should be encouraged to play positive rugby. Always remember that the game is played for enjoyment and, although winning is the priority, to play good attacking rugby should also be your goal. You can attack from anywhere on the pitch and from a variety of situations. However, there are certain guidelines which will help you to choose the right option in a given tactical situation or from a particular area of the pitch, so that you can maximise your attacking potential.

When one talks of 'attacking rugby' it is usually the backs who spring to mind. We have already looked at how an individual might be able to beat his opponent – by a side-step, a swerve or a change of pace. While these individual skills should be encouraged, it is a fact that in modern rugby, fitness and defensive patterns have made it more and more difficult for attackers to break through on their own.

Most attacking moves start from set pieces, such as scrums, line-outs, rucks and mauls, when you can usually count on a supply of ball and have the time to set up a move. Then once they have the ball, the backs can use a range of techniques to break down the opposing defence. They should practise them as a unit.

## Miss-moves and loops

One way of outflanking a defence is to get the ball to the wing very quickly. We have already explained that the ball can travel faster than a man, so by missing out one player in the line the

**1**

To start this attacking move, I miss out the inside centre with my pass, playing the ball straight in front of him.

**2**

The inside centre begins to move out of the line. It is important that he doesn't move too early and give the game away.

ball will obviously reach the wing more quickly. If the full-back has come into the line, either inside or outside the wing, there will be an overlap and the attacking side should be able to gain ground or even score.

Miss-moves are usually carried out between the fly-half and the outside centre, with the inside centre missed out, or between the inside centre and the wing with the outside centre missed out. It is important that the ball is passed flat in front of the man to be missed out. A lobbed pass

will give the defence time to re-adjust and, if the missed-out man begins to move away to create a loop before the ball is passed, the opposition will guess what's happening and cover it.

A miss-move is often accompanied by a loop. Rather than have the missed-out player doing nothing, he can move round the back and re-enter the back line nearer the wing (see pictures on this page). This will once again create an overlap but it must be done crisply and without hesitation to be effective.

A loop can be performed by any two players. A common fault of the loop is that the ball carrier tends to drift across the field and it becomes easier for the defence to shuffle across and snuff out the extra man. It is imperative, therefore, that the player who is looped straightens up when he has the ball, perhaps veering in towards his opposite number, committing him to the tackle. If the man looping the runner comes up on his shoulder to take a short pass, the effect can be devastating.

**3**

As the ball moves down the line, the missed out player runs around the back and into a position outside the wing.

**4**

The ball is played to the inside centre and the loop is complete. The player with the ball should now have space to run into.

### The Scissors

This is one of the most effective ways of creating a gap in the defence and putting a man through it, but it requires excellent timing. It is a technique currently favoured by Bath and England, using forwards scissoring with the backs. Effectively the ball is passed along the line in normal fashion but in a pre-arranged move the man outside the ball carrier comes inside and behind him at an angle. The ball carrier holds the ball in front of him and when the man appears on his inside he gives him the ball (see pictures 1-3).

The idea is to confuse the defenders and create a gap through which the attacker can sprint. Once again it has to be done at pace to be successful. However, the player making the scissors must time his run so that the ball carrier can slow down a fraction, making the pass easier to take. It should be a nice smooth action, and not done at full pace or all kinds of problems will follow: the pass

The scissors: the ball is passed down the line to me. The natural move, at this point, is to pass the ball to the man outside me.

The man who was outside me begins to move inside. He must time his run so that I can slow down and make the pass easy to take.

I pass the ball inside and the scissors is complete. The player with the ball should now find that there is a gap for him to run into.

may be dropped, for example, and the whole attacking momentum lost.

The ball carrier also has the option of a dummy scissors in which he goes through exactly the same sequence except that instead of passing the ball to the man inside he holds onto it and goes on his own. A dummy scissors is often used after a true scissors in order to create confusion and keep the defence guessing, or if the ball is wet and greasy and the ball carrier decides that the situation suddenly is too dangerous for a true scissors.

## Summing up

It is vital in all these moves that the back line is not aligned too deep. If it is, then by the time contact is made with the defence, the defenders will have had time to re-adjust and snuff out the danger.

If possible, the backs should be fairly flat and as near as possible to the gain line (which is an imaginary line running through the middle of a line-out, say, or a scrum as the ball is put in). The closer to the opposition you can put on these moves, the more effective they are likely to be. It is important to remember, too, that in training you are likely to be working in good conditions where the scrum-half and, indeed, all the backs are not under the kind of pressure they may be in matches. In a game situation you must be prepared to work with less than perfect ball and less than perfect passes.

**Jeremy Guscott works a dummy scissors with Simon Halliday in the 1992 England v Romania match.**

For this reason you must always be alert to the changing situation and adjust your play accordingly. It's no use haring off at pace on a loop if the ball has come out slowly; you may well have to adjust your pace or your angle of running in order to receive the ball from your team-mate.

The essential aim in all moves of this sort is to create an element of uncertainty in the opposition. Often you will find that although a move hasn't worked to perfection, it has created enough space for someone to go through. So be prepared to adapt and use your initiative.

---

# Ben's tips

● Most attacking moves come from set pieces. All teams should spend plenty of time practising them.

● Do not expect perfect ball or a perfect pass – you should be prepared to adjust.

● Don't be afraid of trying something new. Even attacking plays that break down can have an unsettling effect on opponents.

## ➡ Attacking from the back row

For forwards like me, involvement in attacking moves tends to centre around the scrum and in particular the back row. The scrum is the one set piece which is ideally suited for set moves off the back row. For one thing, you can be pretty sure of securing the ball on your own put-in and you can also control it. Back-row moves can also be used to suck in defenders so you can re-cycle the ball and exploit an overlap.

Most back-row moves go to the right because that is the natural way for the scrum-half to move after putting the ball into the scrum on the left. By going right you are also taking the ball away from the opposing scrum-half.

The scrum must be solid if you are going to try a move or it may be slightly skewed to the right to provide a little added protection. The quicker the move is done, the more chance you have of success, so try for something simple and don't aim to be too complicated or elaborate.

There is a vast number of moves you can employ using the scrum-half, the No.8 and the two flankers. Depending on where you are on the field, you will either be going for the try-line or looking to punch through the opposition and set up a maul or a ruck.

The simplest move is for the No.8 to pick up the ball and for him to feed the scrum-half who will be coming round on his right. He could also feed one of the flankers or, if the ball were on the blind side near the try-line, the blind-side wing.

Similarly, the scrum-half could make the pick-up behind the scrum and then feed the No.8 or flankers or the blind-side wing. Yet another option is to have one of the back row standing off the scrum and for the scrum-half to use him as a pivot to introduce more variations. Moves

In my role as No.8, I have picked up the ball and broken from the scrum.

I then feed the scrum-half, who has come round on my right.

This is a simple and often very effective attacking move.

**David Campese, one of the most lethal counter-attackers in the game, breaks the Ireland line in the 1991 World Cup quarter-final.**

can also be worked going left, of course, but then you will have to contend with the opposing scrum-half, who will be patrolling that area.

## Counter-attacking

One of the most exciting facets of play in rugby is the counter-attack. This is when, after gaining possession of the ball from a failed move on the part of the opposition, the side defending suddenly launches an attack of their own, usually from deep inside their own half. The easiest option in these circumstances, of course, is the safety-first one of booting the ball out of play, but the side which elects to run the ball can be both entertaining and effective.

It is hard to coach someone to counter-attack. It is very much an instinctive thing but there are certain guidelines which will make the whole process a little less risky. The team

should discuss the benefits and drawbacks of counter-attacking and decide in what circumstances you are likely to run the ball back at the opposition. This way, when a player starts a counter-attack it won't come as a surprise to the rest of the team who may be in a position to help. Counter-attacking is usually the preserve of the full-back or the wings, but anyone can take it upon himself to be adventurous, providing the situation is right.

If you are going to counter-attack then you should make your mind up as soon as you receive the ball. It is vital to maintain the momentum of your attacks. The worst possible scenario after you have fielded the ball is to hesitate until you become hemmed in by opponents and exposed without support. You will probably be tackled and lose the ball, leading to a score for which nobody will thank you.

Even as you are retrieving the ball you will be sizing up the situation, knowing where your own players are and the disposition of the opposition defence. Try to head for an area that can offer you some support and the chance to link up with your team-mates. Try to run straight because the more you run sideways the more difficult it will be for your team-mates to support you.

A good ploy in counter-attacking is to do a switch with either the wing or the full-back. This changes the angle of running and will cause the opposing defence to re-assess their own angles of running.

If you see a team-mate counter-attacking try to get near him to offer support. Set up practices in training to help you to understand the skills of counter-attacking and, as long as everyone knows what you are trying to achieve, then the risk element is greatly reduced.

# Making the ball available

In order to ensure continuity of play and to make the most of possession, every member of the team should know how to present the ball when tackled. Possession is everything in rugby: without the ball you cannot possibly hope to dominate your opponents. When you are tackled you have three options: you can try to pass to a team-mate, you can set the ball up for a maul, or you can set the ball up for a ruck. Securing second-phase possession at both rucks and mauls depends largely on how the tackled player presents the ball. It may seem as though it is difficult to control a tackle situation but it can be done if you learn the right skills and are prepared to practise.

The current laws state that once you are tackled and go to ground then you must release the ball immediately. If you hang on to it you will be penalised, so the trick is to get yourself into a position where you can release the ball in such a way as to make it easier for your team-mates to secure possession.

Much will depend on the tackler and just how he tackles you, but it is possible to manoeuvre him into a

Chris Sheasby, the Harlequin No.8, makes the ball available from a maul in exemplary style during a match against Bath.

position which will give you more options by using footwork and the positioning of your body.

## Passing out of the tackle

The first option when you are tackled is to pass the ball. If, for example, you alter your pace and footwork to make the tackler take you low down, then by carrying the ball high in two hands you will be free to pass to a supporting colleague. As you fall to the ground, slip the ball out and maintain possession.

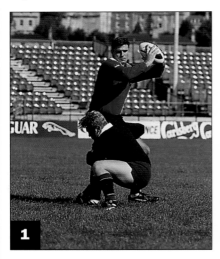

The tackler takes me low down and I hold the ball up to give myself more time.

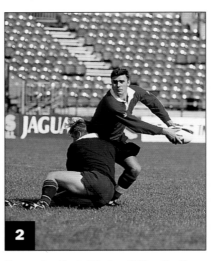

By passing the ball before hitting the floor, I have maintained my team's possession.

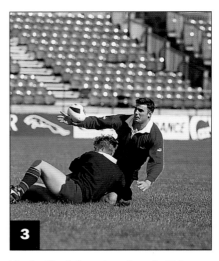

The tackler falls on top of me, but his efforts are in vain; the ball has long gone.

**1**

Faced by an opponent and with no close support my options are limited.

## Turning in the tackle

There will be times when there is no close support so a pass out of the tackle is not going to be possible. And if the tackler hits you higher up on the body he will probably smother your pass, so you must consider retaining your side's possession, perhaps by developing a maul.

Try to use the tackler as a form of support so that you can make the ball available. Once again, it is important to judge your pace and adjust your

footwork to set this up. As you approach the tackler, turn your body around so that your back is hitting his chest.

Your body is now shielding the ball from the tackler and putting it further away from him. Staying on your feet, it is now possible to feed it to a support player who may be able to take it on himself or set up a maul.

**2**

As the tackler approaches, I turn my body so that my back faces his chest.

## Laying the ball back in the tackle

If you think about what you are doing when going into a tackle you should be able to control it; and if you've managed to dictate just how the tackler will take you, then you can manage to put the ball beyond him to create a ruck.

If he takes you low down to the side, you should be carrying the ball in both hands and on impact you can wrap yourself around the tackler's body as you go down. As you hit the ground your upper body will be beyond him and this should enable

you to lay the ball behind him. This presents a clear target for your support players to aim at and they should be able to form a ruck and win the ball. Remember that in a maul situation, you must try to roll away from the ball or you could be penalised. Also, in order to play the ball again you must get up on your feet; you can't scrabble around on the ground.

Of course controlling the ball in the tackle like this takes a lot of practice, but it is the essence of modern, dynamic rugby. If forwards and backs are clear about the principles of controlling the tackles, and can put them into action on the field, then this will make an enormous difference to the team's play. You will have possession of the ball much more. When you are tackled, always try to think of it as an opportunity to set something up rather than as the end of a movement.

**3**

I am now in a better position to stay on my feet and await support.

# The Ruck

**The ruck: it is important for the tackled player to lie in the right position and at the right angle to make the ball easily available.**

**The first man into the ruck should aim to drive beyond the player and the ball on the ground. This drive should claim the ball for the attacking side.**

**If the ball gets stuck you will have to ruck it out with your feet. You cannot use your hands to get the ball back or you will be penalised.**

When the ball carrier is tackled, it is vitally important that his side retains possession. If the player goes to ground with the ball and his team-mates go in to try to retrieve it, a ruck is formed. Rucking is a very important part of the modern game and some teams, such as the New Zealanders, build their whole game around successful rucking.

The ruck is often referred to as a 'second phase' of play – the first phase being the static restarts to the game such as the scrum and the line-out. But where these two set pieces give both sets of forwards time to set themselves up, the ruck is more dynamic and must be organised quickly if it is going to be effective. Also, it is not restricted simply to the forwards. Although they will do the main bulk of the work, backs these days are expected to know what to do when a ruck develops.

Put another way, the ruck is simply a method of securing the ball after a tackle and getting it back to the scrum-half who can then use it to instigate another attacking play. A ruck can be set up deliberately by players as a means of sucking in the opposition's defenders, or it can be simply a result of the ball carrier being tackled. Either way, it is important that the man in possession does the right thing on contact with the tackler. Essentially he goes to ground and his colleagues make a bridge over the ball.

The important elements of a ruck are making the ball available, body position, speed of support and moving the ball away at the right time. Remember that the opposition will be doing their best to drive over the ball and deny you possession.

When the player goes to ground, it is important that he lies in the right position and at the right angle to make the ball most easily available

**All Blacks' back-row forward Zinzan Brooke lays the ball back to enable a ruck to form in a match against the British Lions.**

for his team-mates to come in and get the ball moving again.

Always remember that you have to release the ball as soon as you hit the ground, but the trick is to learn to fall in such a way that you present your own side with a good target. Don't lie over the ball or you will be penalised (and you must remember always to protect your head with your hands).

The first man into the ruck should aim to drive beyond the player and the ball on the ground. The opposition will be there, so this first drive will effectively claim the ball for the attacking side. It is then up to support players, usually the forwards, to grab the shirt of a team-mate and drive in low and hard with their shoulders and force the opposition back.

If you are one of them, you will be aiming to drive over the ball so as to leave it for the scrum-half to set up an attack, but if the ball gets stuck you will have to ruck it out with your feet. Remember, when the ball is on the

ground in a ruck you cannot use your hands to try and get it back or you will be penalised.

Under the current laws it is also imperative that players stay on their feet. Referees are very strict on players who simply dive over the ball and kill it.

The ruck can produce very quick ball if done well and often opposition three-quarters can be sucked into it, which could leave your backs with an overlap if you can get the ball out to them quickly.

Good rucking technique only comes with a lot of practice. It is a

good exercise to use tackle-bags. One man hits the bag, goes down and then the next comes in to bridge over him, making an obvious target so the rest of the forwards have something to aim at.

Remember, rucking is dynamic so don't just amble up and lean on the player in front. And you must have a clear idea what you are going to do when you are at least five metres away.

The laws state that you must join a ruck behind the hindmost player. Adopt a low position and then drive in with your shoulder. Always aim to drive through beyond the ball. Once you have this kind of momentum, going in will be hard to stop. Problems usually occur when players go in too high so going in as low as possible should always be your aim.

Also remember that if the ball gets stuck and doesn't look like coming out, the referee will blow up and order a scrum. The side going forward at the ruck will get the put-in, so it's essential to perfect this area of play.

## Ben's tips

● To be effective, the ruck must be organised quickly.

● When tackled, you should make the ball available for team-mates, presenting them with a good target.

● If you arrive first at a ruck, try to drive beyond the player and the ball.

# The Maul

The maul is another 'second phase' area of play similar to the ruck but the crucial difference here is that the ball is kept in the hand and not put on the ground. As with the ruck, a maul may develop from a player being tackled in possession or it may be the result of a deliberate drive, usually by a forward. Because the ball is in the hand there are more options at a maul and teams have developed several highly effective variations, such as the driving maul and the rolling maul which can be used to great effect. The Australian team showed its mastery of the driving maul in the 1991 World Cup. There have also been significant changes to the laws regarding the maul over recent seasons. But before going on to the variations it is essential to learn the basics.

There are many similarities to the ruck in the approach to the maul. Once again the key elements are a low body position, a good drive and good support. As with the ruck, your decision-making should start about five metres away from the actual maul.

Making the ball available is all important when the ball carrier is tackled. He should try to drive through the tackler by dipping one shoulder and going in low. By leading with the shoulder the ball will be kept away from the tackler.

If the ball carrier goes in high and carries the ball in front of him, it will be easy for the tacklers to rip the ball from his grasp and then they will have the initiative and be able to set up a maul of their own.

It is important for the first players in to set up a platform so that the rest of the forwards have something to aim for and work from. The first player should try to secure the ball while the next two bind either side of him and seal the ball off from the opposition.

Remember that a maul, like a ruck, must be dynamic so you have to

When a player is tackled and stays on his feet, a maul can be formed.

hit it at pace with a low body position and drive it forward. Once the ball has been secured you can either get it out quickly or keep it in waiting for the rest of the support to arrive and drive the opposition back. Players arriving must come in behind the ball and behind the hindmost player or they will be offside. And players must make sure that the channel for the ball is kept clear. Much will depend on how many of the opposition are involved.

Ball presentation – making it available – is vital: you must be able to see the ball at all times. As with the ruck, if the maul was halted then the side going forward used to get the put-in at the ensuing scrum. This is now no longer the case. If the maul grinds

to a halt then the referee will award the put-in at the scrum to the side which did not take the ball in. So the onus is on the side with the ball to make something happen.

While the maul is moving forward there is no problem. But if it is held up or killed the ball must be moved out quickly. The phrase which you may hear referees say is, 'Use it or lose it'. So the emphasis now is on recycling the ball as quickly as possible and keeping the game moving.

The maul is often used as a method of sucking in the opposition's forwards. These days, defences tend to spread out across the field and it is becoming increasingly apparent that many teams do not commit all their forwards to a ruck, but this is not the case with the maul. This is because a maul can be effective very quickly: for example, you can set one up in midfield off a scrum and drive through the heart of the opposition where they are likely to be weaker.

The rolling maul has become a feature of the modern game and involves players shielding one another and continuously moving around the ball. The ball goes through many

## Ben's tips

● When tackled, try to drive through with your shoulder low – this keeps the ball away from the tackler.

● A Maul must be dynamic. If it slows down or comes to a halt, get the ball out quickly.

● Keep driving forward. If you slow down, the opposition will be able to anticipate what is going to happen.

1

The maul has been held up and the red team are forced to take action.

2

The scrum-half has the ball and is looking for a way to use it at this point.

3

As the red team's No.8, I charge into the maul and take the ball from the scrum-half.

**Tackle shields are a lot of fun and can be used to develop maul technique.**

hands so it is essential to keep it as far back as possible from the opposition. If you are in a maul, just keep your team-mates rolling around you.

The trend these days is for a variation of the rolling maul called a 'driving rolling maul'. This is where forwards break off and form mini-packs. The ball is, as always, shielded and secure so that if the move does break down you can form a ruck and whisk the ball away.

It is important to obtain good cohesion among the forwards, so you must know precisely what your job is and what you are trying to achieve. There's not a great deal the opposition can do when you get it right and some teams have been known to move all the way up the pitch with a driving maul, but if you're not proficient at it you will lose a lot of ball.

Don't wait for a maul to come to a halt before you decide what you are going to do because, once you stop, you'll be delivering slow ball and the opposition will know what is going to happen. When you're driving forward they don't.

Most clubs these days use tackle shields to help in developing maul technique. The ball carrier drives into one and turns to set up the ball for the supporting players.

# The Scrummage

**A strong scrum is vital in the modern game – work as a unit and eliminate any weak links that the opposition may exploit.**

The scrum is a method of restarting the game, usually after a knock-on or a forward pass. A scrum is also an option when a ball is not thrown in straight at a line-out; and a side can also decide to take a scrum instead of a penalty.

The scrum has developed over the years into an integral part of the modern game, and players have learned not only to be more effective in winning the ball from the scrum, but also in how to exert such pressure on their opponents that the ball the opposition wins is difficult to use effectively. Sometimes a good pack can win the ball even when it has been put in by the opposing scrum-half: this is called winning the ball against the head.

There is obviously an advantage when your scrum-half is feeding the scrum because he is able to co-ordinate with the hooker, usually by a signal such as a tap on the shoulder, when he wants the ball to be put into the scrum.

The scrum usually consists of all the forwards, packed down tightly together. The front row comprises the hooker in the middle with the two props on either side of him. The one on the left is called the loose-head and the one on the right the tight-head. The second row is made up of the two lock forwards and the back row has the No.8 in the middle and the two flankers on either side.

## Binding

All the players pack down and bind tightly together to form a solid unit. The most important area is the front row. It is the hooker who strikes for the ball and he relies on a solid binding with his props to enable them to support him while he concentrates on striking for the ball. The front rows are the only ones who will actually engage the opposition, so it's essential that they are bound correctly to form a solid unit.

The second-row forwards use their inside arms to bind to each other and their outside arm comes up through their respective prop's legs. A common way of binding is up and onto the waistband of their shorts although you can bring your arm round and grip onto the side of the prop's shorts. The heads of the second row forwards should poke through between the thighs of the props and the hooker. The No.8 puts his head in between the two locks and the flankers bind either side of the locks with their outside arms.

The importance of a strong and solid binding cannot be overemphasised. The tighter you are as a unit, the more effective your scrummage will be. If there is any looseness, this will turn into a weakness when the opposition put pressure on you. It will invariably lead to instability and you will find yourselves losing the ball and being driven backwards in disarray.

**The front row engages the opposition and fights for the ball, so it must be solidly bound.**

**A tight binding of hooker and props is needed for the hooker to do his job properly.**

**The front row has formed a solid unit and will now be joined by the second row.**

### ➡ Winning the ball

In order to win the ball it must first be won by the hooker and then find its way back through the maze of legs to end up in the scrum-half's hands. Although this may sound difficult, it should not be a lottery.

The scrum-half must put the ball in from the left and he can co-ordinate his scrum feed if his hooker taps with his left hand to let him know when he wants the ball to be put in. The hooker must always make sure he is in a comfortable position in which to strike for the ball.

Once the ball is in, it is essential that it is guided through a channel back to the scrum-half. Foot positioning is crucial. You will often hear players talk about Channel-1 and Channel-2 ball at scrums (see diagram). These are the two ways in which the ball should come out of a scrum. Channel-1 ball emerges from between the left flanker and the left-sided lock; Channel-2 ball usually emerges via the No.8's feet.

The choice of channel is important because it will determine what kind of

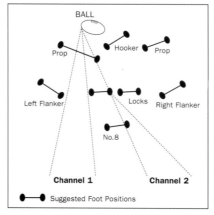

ball the scrum-half gets and what he is able to do with it. Channel-1 ball, because it is using a shorter route with fewer feet to negotiate, provides quicker ball. Although this requires a great degree of precision and an alert scrum-half, it produces such quick ball that it can be a great attacking weapon. The scrum-half can use this ball to make a break himself or get his backs moving much more quickly and the opposition are given less time to read the situation and react.

For Channel-1 ball, the loose-head prop (to the hooker's left) should pack

**In the above picture the hooker has won the ball. He must now direct the ball back to his scrum-half through one of the channels – see diagram, left.**

with his feet fairly wide apart so that, when the hooker strikes, the ball can be guided through his legs. The left-hand lock must make sure that his feet don't interfere with its passage.

Channel-2 ball is more controlled and therefore probably the more common. While it is slower than Channel-1 it is not as risky and therefore is ideal in defensive situations and back-row moves. The ball is worked back to the No.8 who, in conjuction with his scrum-half, will decide what to do with it. If, for example, the ball is very slow coming through, the No.8 may decide to pick it up and drive rather than give his scrum-half bad ball. The scrum-half may decide to put up a kick or pass to his fly-half who may kick, but it is important to decide what you want to do with the ball before it emerges.

While there will be a tremendous temptation only to use Channel-2 ball

**Scrummage machines have made training easier. In the bottom picture on the left, I am checking that the scrum is tightly formed before the unit begins the shove. The resistance offered by a machine like this can be varied to offer different challenges and develop technique.**

because it is comfortable and safe, don't forget about Channel 1. It can give you more options and often take your opponents by surprise.

It is important to practise winning the ball. The timing between scrum-half and hooker is vital: they must build an understanding so that the ball comes in at the right angle and pace.

### The Shove

In addition to winning your own ball, the scrummage can be used to disrupt the opposition and spoil their possession. Scrummaging takes a lot of physical effort and, if you have a better scrummaging unit than the opposition's, it will sap their strength and may also demoralise them.

When the opposition are feeding the scrum, many hookers don't bother to strike for the ball but instead exert pressure on the opposition by going for an eight-man shove.

If a pack gets this right, then it can do enormous damage and put opponents on the defensive. But it's not simply a question of everyone shoving together: each player in the scrummaging unit must have the correct body positions.

It is essential to keep your back straight and your hips low. The locks should push on their props and the flankers need to shove in at an angle on the props. The eight-man shove is effective when timed properly so there's usually a verbal signal at which all the forwards drive in unison.

When the call arrives, you need to drive hard and pull in tight, because the tighter you are, the more effective the drive will be and there will be no wasted energy. Also, make sure that you are pushing in the correct position. Ideally, your shoulder should be at the top of the thigh of the man in front, just below the buttock. If your shoulder is higher it will ride up and over and your push will be ineffective.

The great thing about scrummaging is that it is all about technique. Often a smaller, lighter pack can outscrummage a heavier one because they've got better technique, as the Scottish pack proved in the 1992 Murrayfield game against England.

Scrummage machines have made scrum practice easier. Once the coach has checked everyone is in the correct position, the amount of resistance can be varied to imitate a real pack.

### Ben's tips

● Co-ordination between scrum-half and hooker is crucial when feeding the scrum.

● When the ball is in the scrum it should be guided through a channel to the scrum-half. Choice of channel determines the kind of ball the scrum-half gets.

● A successful eight-man shove depends upon body position — keep your back straight and your hips low.

# The Line-out

The line-out is another method of restarting the game and is adopted after the ball has been kicked into touch. It takes place at the point where the ball crossed the touchline. Because there are far fewer scrums in the game today, and because it is becoming increasingly rare for a side to lose the ball at their own put-in, the line-out has become a significantly more important part of the game. It provides an excellent opportunity to regain possession.

The line-out has had its critics over the years and arguments about it still rage today; it is considered a pretty messy and unruly way of re-starting play. However, it is unique to Rugby Union and has become a vital part of the game. In its simplest terms, the eight forwards from each side line up opposite one another, five metres in from the touchline and one metre apart and the ball is thrown in over the middle of the two lines by the hooker. Only the scrum-half is allowed to be within ten metres of the line-out. All this sounds very simple but coaches and players have looked at every facet closely to try to reduce any element of luck involved in which side gets the ball.

The law-makers too have worked strenuously to clean up the line-out. They have outlawed such things as lifting and using the outside arm to knock back the ball but it remains one of the most difficult areas for the referee to police.

The eight forwards from each side line up opposite each other. Strong and well-organised line-out play can win matches.

The hooker must throw the ball in over the middle of the two lines, but he can vary the ball's pace and flight to benefit his team.

As with the scrum, the line-out is a set piece which requires all the participating forwards to do a specific job, whether jumping, supporting or blocking the opposition, and to do it well. Australia's John Eales and England's Martin Bayfield are particularly adept at securing possession from the line-out. A side which fails to secure consistent possession will find it very difficult to win a match.

## The Throw-in

The spotlight always seems to fall on the jumpers but the most important aspect of the line-out is throwing in. You can have the tallest, most athletic jumpers around but, if the ball does not reach them, their height will be completely redundant.

These days it is down to the hooker to throw in, so he will have to practise long and hard to hone this particular skill. Most hookers employ an American Football type throw, where the ball rotates in the air, for greater accuracy.

There is also a variety of throws the hooker can use to deceive the opposition and get the ball to his preferred jumper. There is the lobbed ball, the fast ball and the long throw to the back. The hooker must find out how the different jumpers want the ball presented to them.

Once the hooker has mastered the mechanics of throwing the ball then he should practice with the various jumpers to get the timing right. In order to help with this co-ordination, teams use a variety of simple and clear coded signals so that everyone in the team will know where the ball is going to go. This means that the support players and the jumper can all act together and everyone is moving in the right direction. Then it's all down to building a relationship between jumper and hooker.

**Brian Moore, the England hooker, throws in during a 1993 Five Nations match. Nowadays the throw-in is a key aspect of the hooker's game.**

## ⇒ Winning the ball

Every player in a line-out is a potential ball winner but the main jumpers tend to be the two locks and the No.8. In today's rugby, positions are even more specialised so that locks classify themselves even further as either a front jumper or a middle jumper. But even those players who are not actively involved in jumping have got an important job to do.

The best way of controlling the ball at a line-out is the two-handed catch. This gives the catcher secure possession and gives his side many options. Once caught, the ball can be fed to the scrum-half or the forward can use it himself to drive or set up a ruck or a maul.

The tap or deflection is the other method which produces quicker ball but, unless it is done correctly, it can lead to all sorts of problems with the ball uncontrolled and the subsequent pass going astray.

Remember that a jumper can only use his inside arm to guide the ball back. Tapping requires timing and co-ordination between the hooker, the jumper and the scrum-half. When all three get it right, the speed with which the ball is won and transferred to the backs can take the opposition by surprise.

Unfortunately, some players see the tap as a soft option and tap wildly. The result is bad ball to the scrum-half who will find himself in difficulty.

### Ben's tips

● Hookers must master a variety of throws and learn how different jumpers like the ball delivered.

● Try a well-controlled tap or deflection. This can get the ball to the backs extremely quickly.

● Support players should bind tightly around the catcher — this creates a shield and keeps the ball secure.

Olivier Roumat, France's giant lock, leaps high to take the ball during the 1993 France v Wales Five Nations match.

I have jumped highest and claimed the ball in the safest way: with both hands.

The line-out obviously favours taller players; however, you don't have to be a giant to be effective. For instance, my Bath team-mate Nigel Redman may be relatively small but he can be devastatingly effective in the line-out. Timing and athleticism can count for a lot and you must have the requisite handling skills to catch the ball in the first place. Foot movement is also important and jumpers should try to be light on their feet.

With specific training, the height of your jump can improve but it must also be remembered that the line-out is a physical confrontation, so you must be tough and strong in order to succeed. Having the right kind of determination and aggression can often win the day over supposedly physically superior opponents.

## Support play

Once the jumper has gained possession, everyone else, including the hooker, becomes a support player. The ball must be protected because the opposition will storm through the line and try to turn it into bad possession.

Those players immediately next to the catcher should bind on him, facing the opposition to provide an effective shield for the ball carrier. All the other players now have a target to aim for and they bind on to secure the ball and prevent the opposition breaking through. The closer and tighter they bind, the more secure the ball will be.

This is the kind of practice which must be done in training until it becomes second nature and everyone is aware of their job. Because of the nature of the line-out, the ball will often squirt out at all angles so every player must be prepared to adapt. Securing the ball is vital and supporting the ball winner is crucial.

## Short line-outs

A line-out can be made up of any number of players between two and eight. Short line-outs are a variation and can prove extremely effective in certain situations and give teams another option.

They can be used to re-cycle possession quickly and gain second-phase possession. They can also be employed if a team finds it is making no headway in the full line-out. By cutting the numbers it just might throw the opposition out of their stride. Cutting the line-out also creates space.

There is plenty of variety which can be employed in the line-out. Moving your main jumpers around will always keep the opposition guessing. If you are being beaten consistently, do not be afraid to experiment with different combinations and line-out lengths – you have nothing to lose.

**Good line-out support play is critical if you are to make the most of your possession at the throw-in. The players next to the catcher should protect him from the opposition.**

**Short line-outs can be extremely effective and can get the ball back in play quickly.**

# Kicking

Although rugby is primarily a handling game, kicking is an integral part of it. Everyone should understand the mechanics of kicking, although it is the backs who will do most of it, and in particular the fly-half and the full-back.

There are many different types of kick, from place-kicks and drop-kicks through to punting and grubber-kicks. Although all are different there are certain basic principles which are the same for each and have to be adhered to. You have to keep your eye on the ball all the time, hit the ball cleanly when you kick and then follow through smoothly.

First, let us look at the punt. In modern rugby you will find that most balls are made from a synthetic material which helps to repel water. This, coupled with the fact that there have also been advances in the technique of kicking, enables modern kickers to send the ball much greater distances than their predecessors ever imagined would be possible.

When kicking to touch, most players these days opt for the screw-kick. This means kicking the ball at a slight angle so that it rotates rather like a screw as it cuts through the air. To do this, hold the ball at an angle before you kick it and your boot must make contact in such a way as to impart spin.

First, hold the ball correctly. Once you have decided where you're going to kick it, it is necessary to address the ball. For a kick with the right foot, hold the ball out at a slight angle with your right hand on top of it, at the end nearest to you, and the left hand on the side at the further end of the ball.

It is important that the ball is 'placed' rather than just dropped on the boot because the more control you have over it before you strike it, the more likely it is to be lying at the

**Preparing to kick with the right foot. The ball must be at the right angle when kicked.**

correct angle when you make contact. Never toss the ball up before kicking and swing at it. This increases the margin for error and you will be extremely lucky to make good contact.

Make sure the ball is held at a comfortable distance in front of you. You don't want to be too cramped but you don't want to find yourself having

to stretch for it. You should be looking to guide the ball onto your boot, keeping it as steady as possible.

In order to impart the spin which will enable the ball to screw through the air, aim to hit it low down with the outside of your foot. Hitting it at an angle should cause it to torpedo through the air. You need to keep your head down and make clean

The toe of your boot should end up pointing in the direction of the ball and your follow-through should be full.

Neil Jenkins, the Wales fly-half, keeps his eye firmly on the ball before kicking.

contact. The toe of the boot should end up pointing in the direction of the ball and you should have a full follow-through.

It may seem difficult to get the ball to spin at first, so go on practising until you discover the right angle of contact. Don't be too ambitious when you start; just go for short distances until you get the feel of the ball and the spin.

Similarly, in a match, don't be too ambitious with your first kicks, particularly if you're in a position where you'll be kicking a lot. Your team would much rather you make a fifteen-metre touch than a thirty-metre attempt which just fails and results in the opposition fielding the ball. As the game progresses and your confidence builds, you can try longer kicks.

You will have to practise long and hard to become a good kicker and fortunately it's something you can do on your own. But when you do practise, rather than just booting the ball aimlessly, try to make the exercise game-related.

So try touch-finders from the positions you would find yourself in during a match, just inside your own 22 and fifteen metres in from touch, for example, or on your own try-line just five metres in from touch. Remember that you can only kick direct to touch from inside your own 22 or from a penalty. Try some kicks from the centre of the field and work out which touch, right or left, you find it easier to aim at. Also practise kicking from outside your own 22 where you have to bounce the ball into touch.

Most players have a favoured foot but increasingly top kickers can kick with both feet. This is something you should try because there are going to be situations when it is almost impossible to use your favoured foot.

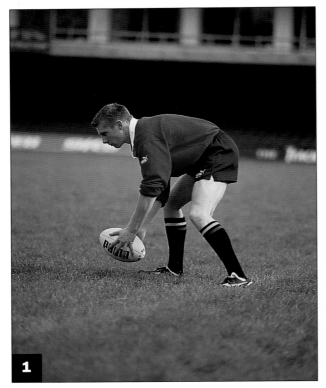

**1**

The box-kick: the scrum-half picks the ball up from the scrum.

He kicks the ball high and deep into the corner of the field.

**2**

## ➡ The Box-kick

This is essentially a scrum-half's weapon and can be of great tactical value. It involves picking up from the scrum and punting the ball to the blind-side, usually deep into a corner. The kick needs to be high enough to enable your three-quarters, who will have been told what to expect, to set off in pursuit and put pressure on whoever may gather the ball. All the great scrum-halves of the world use this to great effect – for example, Robert Jones's memorable box-kicking in the 1989 Wales v England game. Again, it is something which must be practised until you can gauge the weight and distance of the kick you need.

## The Up-and-under or 'garryowen'

The high steepling kick to the full-back or wing has become a popular tactic in modern rugby. The higher the kick, the more time your team-mates have to get under it and put the catcher under pressure or even to catch it themselves.

The principles of the punt remain the same, although usually you need much more height instead of distance. Once again, it is essential to keep your head down, make a clean contact with the ball and follow through smoothly.

## Drop-kick

Being able to drop-kick is a vital part of the kicker's role. Drop-kicks are used to re-start the game after scores and also from the 22 after the ball has gone dead behind the goal. You can also score points with a successful drop-kick at goal. Each kick requires

Right: Michael Lynagh, Australia's fly-half and record international points scorer, shows the clean kicking technique so important to Australia's recent success.

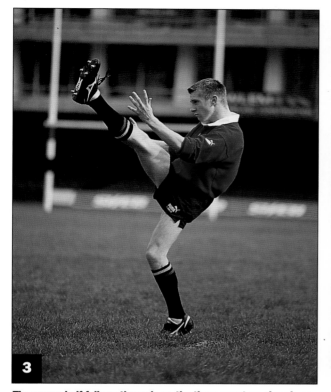

3

The scrum-half follows through, as the three-quarters give chase.

Eric Elwood, Ireland's fly-half, punts the ball for touch.

something different. A drop-out from the 22 merely has to cross the line so you will be looking for height but not a great deal of distance. Re-starts from the halfway line have to travel at least ten metres and you will want to give your forwards the opportunity to contest the ball so you will need height and distance. For a drop-goal you will be looking for a long straight kick with plenty of height.

Drop-kicking is all about timing. The principles are that you line up the ball straight with your hands out in front, guide it down to your boot and, as soon as it makes contact with the ground, strike it. Most kickers these days kick in the round-the-corner style where the instep or laces part of the boot makes contact as if you were hitting a soccer ball. The advantage of this method is that, with more of your boot in contact with the ball, there is less margin for error.

It is essential with the drop-kick not to be distracted by looking to where you hope the ball will land. Once you have picked your target, concentrate on the point at which your boot is going to strike the ball. Don't drop the ball from too great a height – it's not necessary and increases the margin for error. You should be looking for an action that is neat and compact, as Stuart Barnes did when he drop-kicked the winning goal with ten seconds to go in the Bath v Harlequins 1993 Pilkington Cup final.

When drop-kicking for goal, in particular, try to block everything out to concentrate on your kicking routine. Forget what stage the game is at or how near the tacklers are. If you practise hard enough the technique will become ingrained and the steps automatic so that you won't get flustered.

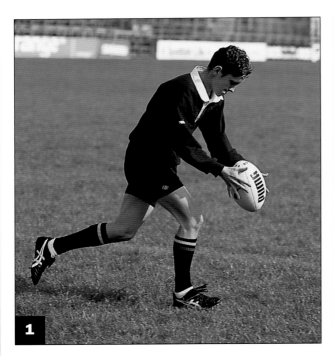

## ➡ The Grubber-kick

The grubber-kick is an effective and popular tactical kick. It is basically a short kick, often played into space, which travels along the ground for approximately fifteen to twenty metres. It can be particularly useful if the opposing defence is standing flat and coming up quickly; and when hit diagonally for your winger, it can create clear scoring opportunities. A good example of this is Jeremy Guscott's 1989 try for the Lions against Australia which was the direct result of a grubber-kick.

To execute the kick place the ball in front of you with your fingers lined up straight, and lean over the ball as you guide it onto your foot. At the point at which the ball strikes the ground, you should kick through it so that it rolls or bounces along the ground.

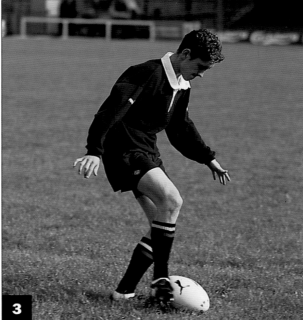

## Place-kicking

Place-kicking has improved dramatically over the years and you have only to look at how many games are decided by kicks to realise just how important it is today. Better

**The grubber-kick: keep your eyes on the ball and strike through it as it hits the ground.**

quality balls and the introduction of kicking tees or sand has made life even easier. Once again, most modern kickers favour a soccer style round-the-corner action.

The first priority is to raise the ball up clear of the ground. This is usually done with a plastic tee or with sand; otherwise the kicker will have to make his own tee by digging in with the heel of his boot. Once the ball is placed clear of the ground, line it up to point in the direction in which you want it to go. Then take a few measured paces backwards. The length of run-up does not correspond with the distance you are going to kick; it depends entirely on what makes you feel most comfortable.

Before you begin your run-up, take one last look at the spot between the posts where you intend to kick the ball and then concentrate on the point of the ball with which you are going to make contact. Then keep your eyes fixed on that point.

It is usually necessary for kickers to take one or two paces to the side in order to approach at the right angle. The run up should be as smooth and straightforward as possible. The more rhythmic it is and free of unnecessary jerks, the easier it will be to develop the timing that is so essential to successful kicking.

Kicking is all about timing, co-ordinating all the actions smoothly and to maximum effect. This is why many of the best kickers are only slightly built. Their timing is so good that it compensates for their lack of physical strength.

The non-kicking foot should be placed just behind and to the side of the ball, and the head should be kept down at all times with the foot swinging smoothly through the ball.

Adjustments and allowances may have to be made for the wind, but these are things that will come naturally once you begin to kick regularly. With kicking, the importance of practice cannot be overemphasised; the top kickers practise nearly every day. If your opportunities are limited to organised team coaching sessions, try to reach the ground a little early or stay late to practise your kicking.

## Ben's tips
● Don't be too ambitious at first – wait until your confidence builds before trying a more difficult kick.
● Keep your head down and your eye on the ball so that you make a clean contact. Follow through smoothly.
● Frequent practice is essential. Practise kicking with both feet.

Develop a smooth and straightforward run-up, as this will help with your timing.

Keep your eyes fixed on the point of the ball that you are going to strike.

Keep your head down and swing your foot smoothly through the ball.

# Fitness

Rugby is a physically demanding sport. Those who play it must have speed, strength, stamina and suppleness if they are to make the most of their ability. Fortunately, the days are long gone when training was seen as something for fanatics. To make the most of your attributes and to gain the most pleasure from the sport you will need to be fit.

You must become fit for rugby and not simply use the game as a means of becoming fit. While there is no substitute for playing, you can go a long way to prepare yourself for the contest before you step out on to the pitch.

What are the fitness requirements for rugby? Being fit for one sport does not mean you will be fit enough to play another. An athlete may be fit for a marathon but he would not be fit to play rugby and vice versa; the requirements are totally different.

Being fit for a particular sport means that you should be able to play it to the best of your ability and in a way that gives you the maximum amount of pleasure. But rugby is complex because each of the fifteen different positions on the field may require different types of fitness.

**Victor Ubogu, the England prop, during a fitness training session in Lanzarote, 1993.**

For example, a wing will need a sprinter's pace and the stamina to do repeated runs, but he will also need a certain strength to be able to make a tackle and take a tackle. A prop will need a lot of upper body strength and the kind of stamina that will allow him to scrummage for eighty minutes.

The most significant thing about rugby is that it is a collision sport. You have people running into one another at high speed. Receiving tackles and making tackles can take a lot out of you and you must have the strength to withstand these hits and still carry on.

Rugby differs from, say, American Football because you are on the field all the time. As both teams become tired towards the end of the game, this often becomes the crucial period. As players slow down, gaps emerge and tackles are missed and the fitter of two evenly matched sides will probably win.

It is no use being a brilliant runner or having a great side-step if you get exhausted after a couple of runs. Once you become fatigued your reactions slow down and your decision-making becomes impaired. So the fitter you are, the better you will be able to play the game.

More and more clubs these days not only have a qualified coach but also a fitness adviser. A team's fitness programme will almost certainly start during the off-season for it is then that the team and the individual players can start to build a solid base. Once the season has started, the coaching sessions should concentrate on skills and practices, with regular match play keeping the players basically fit. Even so, each individual should have a fitness programme taking care of stamina, the development of upper body strength, weight training, sprinting and so on.

**Gavin Hastings shows the value of sprint training on the 1993 British Lions tour.**

## Sprinting

It is often said in rugby that there is no answer to pace. If someone is quicker than you then nine times out of ten he should beat you. But you can improve your sprinting speed by developing a good stride pattern and using your arms. The pumping of the arms is one of the key facets in running. You should also try to develop a smooth, balanced running action.

The most important asset in rugby is speed off the mark. It's no use being a world-beating sprinter if it takes you fifty metres to get into top gear. Most players, particularly three-quarters, need speed over twenty-five metres, so you should bear this in mind when training.

⇒ Generally, acceleration over the first ten metres is what you should aim for, going from a standing start to full speed in as little time as possible. It is important to get into your stride quickly and you can work on this.

Also try sprinting from a kneeling start or sitting on the floor, perhaps even facing the wrong way. These are the positions you will find yourself in on a rugby pitch, so if you can train with this in mind then it will be of enormous benefit.

## Suppleness

Rugby involves getting your body into all kinds of odd positions. The more supple you are, the better you will be able to cope. Forwards, in particular, should work on their mobility because scrummaging and line-out work, and also rucks and mauls, need bodies that can easily adapt.

Ideally, you should put together a set of exercises which works on all the muscle groups and joints which you are likely to need. Develop a routine of going through each one, gently stretching.

Make sure you don't bounce when you're at full stretch or do any excessive jerks. It should be a gentle progression until you feel the muscle or the joint is fully stretched, then after holding that position for a few seconds, relax.

Do these exercises as part of your warm-up before a match or a training session. Failure to warm up properly can lead to muscle strains and tears, so give yourself enough time to go through your routine fully.

## Weight training

All players, not just forwards, will benefit from a proper programme of weight training. Although the needs of the forwards are obvious, upper body strength more and more

**Suppleness: you can do all these exercises (1-7) as part of your warm-up before a match. Don't forget: rugby is a physically demanding sport and those who play it must train and practise hard to develop speed, strength, stamina and suppleness.**

**Failure to warm up properly before a match can lead to muscle strain and tears so give yourself enough time to go through your routine fully. The more supple your body is, the better you will be able to cope with the rigours of the match.**

means the difference between breaking tackles and being stopped or retaining possession instead of losing it.

Weight training should be an essential part of your pre-season training programme because it is here that you will build a solid base which will take you through the season. More and more clubs are now installing gymnasiums or at the very least have weight-training rooms. But, lacking a gym, you can always make up your own weights at home to enable you to train more effectively.

However, it is important, especially for youngsters, to have expert advice when it comes to devising a suitable programme. The wrong type of exercise can have a damaging effect on growing bones so you must ensure that you are doing the right type of exercise with the right type of weights.

**The Sprints** Mark a spot ten metres away from your exercise point. On the completion of each exercise sprint to it and back again. Don't stop and rest until the sixth sprint on each set. Remember: everything must be done at full match pace.

Here are the six exercises:

**1 Curls** Keep your elbows by your

side and pump your arms to the full extent of their movement up and down. This exercise will increase strength and endurance for mauling. In the second half you'll be ripping the ball from weakening opposition.

**2 Shoulder Press** Shoulder strength rather than bulk is essential for coming out best in contact

situations. And, combined with leg strength and good technique, shoulder strength can help to make crunching tackles.

**3 Straight Arm Raises** Keep your arms straight and you will feel your muscles 'burn' well before the last set. This helps me to get that extra

### ➡ Ben's match fitness circuit

Long runs and heavy weights are the last things I personally would want to take on to my training schedule in mid-season. So I suggest you try this short, sharp circuit that prepares speed, upper body endurance, heart and lungs for playing and leaves you fresh to give one hundred per cent effort during a match.

Fitness experts have devised an aerobic work-out for me using light weights (they shouldn't be heavier than five kilos) that can be adapted to any rugby player's schedule. Thirty fast repetitions of each of these six

exercises punctuated with explosive twenty-metre sprints reproduces the demands of the toughest match. Do three sets, with two minutes' rest between each.

Four important points to remember are:

**1** Always warm up with a jog and then stretch for at least five or ten minutes.

**2** Maintain speed and quality.

**3** Fully extend your arms in each exercise.

**4** Warm down and stretch when you finish.

jumping height in the line-out and gives me more strength to keep the ball once I have caught it.

**4 Lateral Swing** Chest, shoulders and back work together. Decrease

the weights or even drop them completely for the last set if either your speed or the quality of each exercise is suffering.

**5 Running Arms** This one will help increase your acceleration and will

take you through tackles. Stronger arms give you better balance when moving fast and improve the effectiveness of your hand-off.

**6 Wrists** Strength and endurance in your wrists and forearms are the key to ball retention and control.

Every player on the field needs to do this one, especially tight-binding front fives.

Repeat this circuit once or twice a week between team-training sessions

and games and you will start to feel much sharper throughout the season. To maintain speed and quality, tailor the session to suit your own special needs.

## Summing up

Not many players look forward to fitness training because it can be repetitive and boring, but it does not need to be. With plenty of variation the sessions can be enjoyable. Remember, the hardest decison is simply having to decide whether or not to attend. Once you have decided to go, just get on with it and look forward to the satisfaction you will feel afterwards.

# Ben Clarke factfile

**B**enjamin Bevan Clarke was born in Bishop's Stortford, Hertfordshire, on April 15, 1968. His father Bevan had always been involved in rugby and became chairman of the local club, Bishop's Stortford RFC.

Although Ben played rugby at school it wasn't his number-one sport and it was at swimming that he first represented Hertfordshire. However, when he started playing rugby for the local club he soon began to impress and gained honours, representing Hertfordshire Colts, the Under-21 team, and finally the full County team while still with Bishop's Stortford.

But it wasn't long before Ben attracted the attention of bigger clubs and he joined Saracens at the start of the 1990/91 season. He was selected to play for the London Division in the Divisional Championships that season and toured Australia with them in the summer of 1991.

Ben was then invited to join Bath, the top English club, and his career really began to take off. In 1992 he played in the England B side which beat Spain, Ireland B, France B and Italy B and toured with them to New Zealand.

He made his full England debut against South Africa at Twickenham in the autumn of 1992 when England gained an historic 33-16 win. An ever-present for England in the 1993 Five Nations Championship, Ben's performances secured him a place on the British Lions tour to New Zealand that summer.

That tour was a personal triumph for Ben. He impressed the New Zealanders, the most discerning rugby followers in the world, with some wonderful performances and regards the Lions' win against the All Blacks in the second Test as one of the high spots of his rugby career.

However, the All Blacks took that Test series 2-1 and it was not until the autumn of 1993 that England gained their revenge, when they beat New Zealand at Twickenham in a magnificent game in which Ben played an important part. Although

England could not match that form in the 1994 Five Nations Championship, Ben featured in Bath's 'double' triumph when they convincingly retained their Courage first division title and then beat the league runners-up, Leicester, in the final of the Pilkington Cup, played before a world record crowd for a club match of 68,000.

In the summer of that year Ben toured South Africa with England and collected a try in their superb 32-15 victory over the Springboks in Pretoria. In England's final international of 1994, against Canada, Ben once again showed his versatility by reverting to open-side flanker and played a storming game.

Ben is one of the giants of modern rugby. He is strong and athletic and at 6ft 5in and just under 17 stone he is the perfect size for an international forward. In an era when positions have become inceasingly specialised, Ben is unique in that he is extremely versatile and has played in all three back-row positions at the

Ben powers forward during Bath's 14-6 defeat of Leicester which put the 1994 Courage Championship beyond all doubt.

very highest level. Although he prefers No.8, he has filled both the blind-side and open-side wing forward positions with distinction. In New Zealand in 1993 he was voted one of the players of the year and in 1994 became the overwhelming choice of the *Rugby World* readers for their player-of-the-year award.

Ben is a dynamic player, an explosive runner who can turn a game with bursts of power and aggression. He roams freely around the pitch and is devastating with the ball in his hands. He also reads the game well and can link up with both backs and forwards.

But Ben doesn't neglect the defensive side of his duties and his tackling is extremely effective. He has the knack of knowing when to tackle the ball carrier round the legs or wrap him up in a smother tackle and is a more than useful addition to the line-out.

**Ben leads the attack for the Lions against the All Blacks in the third Test in 1993.**

Dick Best, the former England coach, now Harlequin's director of rugby, has said of him: 'Anyone who can play at Nos.6, 7 and 8 at international level must be phenomenally good. Ben continues to get better and better wherever he plays and has the priceless ability to always be on hand close to the ball.'

Ben had ambitions to be a farmer and went to the Royal Agricultural College at Cirencester but he now works in public relations with National Power in Swindon.

**Ben, just recognisable on the ground, scores England's second try in their 20-8 defeat of Ireland in the 1995 Five Nations game.**

# Ben's dream team

**Nick Farr-Jones: the inspiration behind Australia's World Cup success in 1991.**

During my career I have played against and watched some fine rugby players. The following have impressed me with their skills, ability and attitude, and they are all a credit to the game.

**15  André Joubert**, the Springboks' dashing full-back, had an outstanding tour of Wales and Scotland in 1994 and emerged as one of the world's best full-backs.

**14  David Campese** of Australia has scored more Test tries than any other player and was voted the 1991 World Cup player-of-the-tournament. He has outstanding flair and intelligence and reads the game better than most .

**13  Jeremy Guscott** first played for England in 1989 and has represented the British Lions in five Tests. Now recovered from injury, he should make and score many more points for England.

**12  Philippe Sella** has won over 100 caps for France and has taken part in all three World Cups to date.

His experience and rugby intelligence make him a must for any side.

**11  Rory Underwood** made his England debut in 1984 and since then has taken part in six Tests for the British Lions. His tremendous fitness and exceptional pace remain quite remarkable.

**10  Michael Lynagh** is Australia's captain and the world's leading international points scorer with 813. He is an outstanding play-maker and I can think of no better stand-off in world rugby.

**9  Nick Farr-Jones** retired as Australia's captain and scrum-half in 1992 after winning a total of sixty-three caps, leading his country to a great victory in the 1991 World Cup and having shared with Michael Lynagh the world record half-back partnership of forty-seven games together.

**Laurent Cabannes: a joy to watch, but a handful to play against.**

**8 Tim Gavin** is perhaps the most talented No.8 in world rugby. Formerly a lock, he first played for Australia in 1988. Since then, only a serious knee injury has interrupted his international career.

**7 Laurent Cabannes**, the openside flanker for Racing Club and France, is the second Frenchman in my side. He is one of the most skilful and athletic loose forwards in the game.

**6 Tim Rodber** began his international career for England at No.8 and switched to blind-side flanker two years later. He is a courageous player, fearless and totally committed.

**5 John Eales**, Australia's giant lock, had highly successful debut seasons in both 1991 and 1992. Unfortunately, a shoulder injury put him out of action throughout 1993 but if he has made a full

Victor Obogu: powerful and athletic, a revelation in England's 1995 Grand Slam team.

recovery, he should again be a forceful presence in the line-out for Australia in 1995.

**4 Martin Johnson**, would be a formidable line-out partner for Eales. His eighteen months spent playing in New Zealand broadened his game tremendously and he has scarcely put a foot wrong for England since then.

**3 Victor Ubogu** can play on either side of the scrum, though he prefers tight-head. Since Probyn's retirement, Victor has played outstandingly well for England, the pack inspired by his enormous strength and exuberance.

**2 Phil Kearns** was virtually unknown when he was selected to hook for the Wallabies in 1989. But he has remained in the Australian line-up ever since, and has captained the side in Lynagh's absence.

**1 Jason Leonard**, the loose-head prop, made his debut for England in 1989 and has played in three Tests for the British Lions. He is a dedicated player, solid as a rock, and one of the best props in rugby.

Phil Kearns: a consistent and effective player for the Wallabies.

# Index